The Abstract Vessel

Forms of expression & decoration by nine artist-potters

Gordon Baldwin

Alison Britton

Ken Eastman

Philip Eglin

Elizabeth Fritsch

Carol McNicoll

Jacqui Poncelet

Angus Suttie

Betty Woodman

Ceramics in Studio

John Houston

Bellew Publishing

Oriel / Welsh Arts Council

First published in Great Britain in 1991 by
Bellew Publishing Company Limited in collaboration
with Oriel/Welsh Arts Council

Bellew Publishing Company Limited
7 Southampton Place, London WC1A 2DR

Copyright © John Houston 1991

Designed by Ray Carpenter

ISBN 0 947792 71 6

Half title page: Angus Suttie Drawing 1990

1. Philip Eglin (Frontispiece)
'Venus et Amour' 1989 earthenware
height 24in (61cm)

*The works illustrated and those included
in the exhibition are from private
collections, from the artists, and from*

Crafts Council
Galerie Francesca Pia, Bern,
   Switzerland
Anne and Tim Roberts
Ed Wolf

Photographic Credits

(references are to caption numbers)
Gordon Baldwin 17, 18
Geoff Brightling/Crafts Council 1
David Cripps 5-8, 11, 15, 16, 23-29,31
Philip Eglin 30, 32
Tim Hill 9
Angus Suttie 10
David Ward 12-14, 19-22
John White front cover 2, 3, 4

Printed by Eagle Colourbooks Ltd. Scotland.

Boat
shoe
hat
spoon
box
cup
can
spout
body
chest
squat
bucket
hod
trunk
case
cart
tank
skip

Contents

Alison Britton Drawing / words 1988

Foreword

THE ABSTRACT VESSEL is the fundamental image of this century's ideas about pottery as an art. It is the apt title of this book and of the exhibition from which the book has grown. Both events are based on the work of the same nine artists. They choose to be potters; they are also interpreters. In this book their artifacts are categorized as fiction and discussed in the context of poetic thought. In contrast to utilitarian pots, these objects are slowly, thoughtfully built from very personal raw material — the complex imagining of what pottery could be. The function of these pots, as the book suggests, is to provide diverse explanations of their own nature.

Since the early years of this century, the concept of pure abstract essence has been a profound and helpful basis within the visual arts. In 1930 the critic Herbert Read praised pottery as pure art, and as the will to form's most free expression and most abstract essence. His statement, which is quoted in full in this book, forged a useful link for artist-potters with the meanings and language of Modernism.

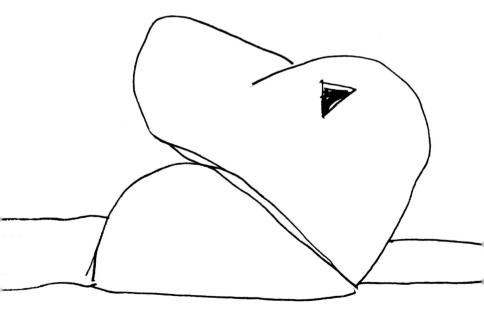

Sixty years later these nine artist-potters work with a language which has absorbed Modernism's processes and practices. But those purist abstractions have been complicated and enriched with a lively vocabulary of ornament, decoration and imaginative embellishment. What unites the work of these artist-potters — and was a prime reason for exhibiting them together — is an interest in decoration as an active means of their expression. Decoration is an eloquent means for these potters; not just a way to make a decorative object, it is part of the complex of references, contradictions, and interactions which shape the forms and paint and inscribe the surfaces of these abstract vessels.

The Abstract Vessel is the title of the exhibition which was first shown at **Oriel,** the Welsh Arts Council's gallery in Cardiff, from 5 April to 4 May 1991, and later went on tour in the United Kingdom. Our grateful thanks are due to John Houston for his informed text, and to the artists and lenders whose generosity has made possible both the exhibition and this book.

Jenni Spencer-Davies, Head of Gallery, **Oriel,** Cardiff
Ralph Turner, Curator of the Exhibition

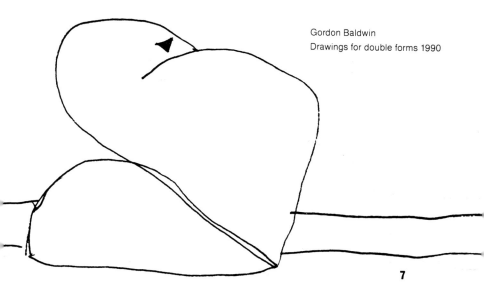

Gordon Baldwin
Drawings for double forms 1990

Ken Eastman Drawing 1990

"A poeticized culture would be one which would not insist we find the real wall behind the painted ones, the real touchstones of truth as opposed to touchstones which are merely cultural artifacts. It would be a culture which, precisely by appreciating that all touchstones are such artifacts, would take as its goal the creation of ever more various and multicolored artifacts."

Richard Rorty: *Contingency, Irony, and Solidarity*
(Cambridge University Press, 1989)

THE POT'S THE THING! These artist-potters know that they have to invent their objects; make them up, as children do stories, out of past events made vivid with new feeling. Making sense of experience is, because of pottery's protracted techniques, a long slow process. Large tracts of the hand-made pottery world have been semi-automated for millenia, with the potter's wheel encouraging the repetition of hollow forms and so becoming the motivating force behind the fact and the idea of the container. The fiction of social fact exists as an aesthetic which is still tuned to forms and functions that make meaning out of ingenious modulations of the 'ordinary' and the 'useful'. These highly privileged words endorse a special role and place for such pottery; it's a friendly everyday legend in which familiar forms are the shape of domesticated presence; its protective nature — as container, as conserver — unites it with the idea and the fact of the house, the home, the prime container. Within that psychological space of the home, such pots can be powerful fictions, furnishing each room with ideas.

Artist-potters are able to step in and step out of the river of 'ordinary' production. In fact, all but a few stay very close to its nature — its various natures, as interpreted by them, becoming faithful commentaries on the true source of all pottery objects. Fortunately, it is a colossal river, able to receive all homage without much alteration. Most potters are glad and grateful to be part of this unending tradition and

9

2. Betty Woodman
'Still Life Vase #6' 1990
earthenware
height 32in (81cm)

3. Betty Woodman
'Peony Shelf Vase Bouquet'
1989 earthenware
height 34in (86cm)

proudly feel themselves to be part of its apparently unchanging nature. Indeed the relationship is formed upon the fact that pottery can be described so plainly in terms of 'natural' forces and substances. Clay, rock, water, fire: they continue to keep pottery close to creation myths; even our modern social nature continues to invest the hand-made with metaphoric meanings. Pots and other artifacts can represent Nature humanized: matter bearing witness to its own transformation by means of a thousand tiny fingerprints.

But are the meanings of all modern pots so generalized, so dissolved in a single mighty stream that has been flowing since prehistoric times? Our perception of the past may emphasize continuity, but the most searching modern work seems to favour abstract qualities that can be defined and debated in the languages of Modernism. At one level, that of the contextualising clues that establish the genre of the object, these languages are interestingly disruptive because they were originally developed within other arts — architecture, sculpture and painting being the prime examples. The crafts have in the last twenty years plundered Modernism as an unprotected site of art styles and stratagems; the plunder has mostly been used for dressing up, for decorating objects with a knowing gesture towards other arts: one of the traditional gossipy roles for the applied arts. But disruption is another matter, one that is relished by some of these artist-potters as they adopt and adapt these languages. There are welcomed degrees of incongruity and awkwardness in the work of Jacqui Poncelet, Alison Britton, Carol McNicoll and Philip Eglin; matters of stance and articulation where the artist's voice and the potter's form do not quite match; where the language is vivid but not entirely pottery-compatible: not authorized by pottery past.

At this point the abstract vessel begins to be re-invented, made up, re-filled with more than the usual concerns of pottery. But those usual concerns are given an honourable place, praised for *being* innocent and humble (see Yanagi's hymn to 'commonest crockery' in the next section) or artfully *performed* (one thinks of a Method actor exploring the character's motives) as felicitous awkwardness, spontaneous dints and dribbles, as marks of deliberate haste on slowly made objects. Not quite quotation, but certainly part of the anecdotal mix of languages and gestures; visual conversations with structures and rhythms that proceed with areas of both clarity and ambiguity. These are canny artifacts; many of them planned to avoid single-mindedness, with plans and elevations that play with space and shuffle intervals; most importantly, their size and asymmetry makes the observer move to search out each object's different views. Abstract vessels certainly, but so rich in metaphors and analogies that our mental contexts are figured with a montage of kindred inventions, constructions, fictions — object-poems improvised in a cluster of hybrid tongues.

Alison Britton
Drawings and words 1988

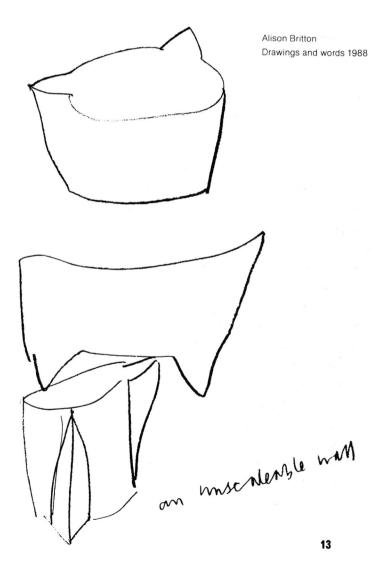

an unscrutable wall

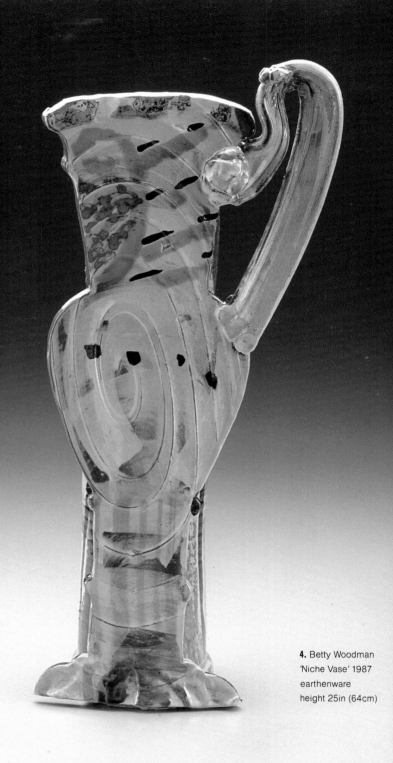

4. Betty Woodman
'Niche Vase' 1987
earthenware
height 25in (64cm)

5. Alison Britton
'Tall Blue and White'
1983 earthenware
height 14in (36cm)

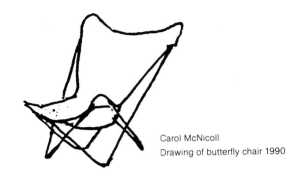

Carol McNicoll
Drawing of butterfly chair 1990

"You must discard the word Fancy altogether. You have nothing to do with it. You are not to have, in any object of use or ornament, what would be a contradiction in fact."

Mr Gradgrind instructing the schoolchildren in
Charles Dickens's *Hard Times* (1854)

"As the age-long traditions of craftsmanship and structural design, which had lingered on from the middle ages, finally faded out under the impact of the new industrialism, the amateur stepped in, his brain teeming with fancies. Craftsmanship was dead ..."

Roger Fry: *The Ottoman and the Whatnot* (1919)

Humdrum Fact or Fancy Fiction?

What are these objects? Human activity is a self-defining process: every made *thing* has meaning, is a representation of the maker's concerns and, willy-nilly, probably represents much else besides. Objects are made out of human nature, out of our social, hopeful, remembered selves. All artifacts are fictions however much we may hope they can be true or natural, or wish that they might exist in some safe and serious dimension, beyond doubt and criticism. On New Year's Day 1991, the British Chancellor of the Exchequer was challenged to reveal the meaning behind his plans for the economy. Accused of repeating dull platitudes, he responded sharply, saying that he was not writing a novel or a play; his task was humdrum – a word he used several times to try to distance himself from fiction's flights of fancy. The implication was clear: the world of politics and economics was real; serious, factual and commonplace. No connection with the world next door.

Philip Rawson seems to agree. His essay 'Empty Vessels' (in *Fast Forwards*, 1985, book of the exhibition at the Institute for Contemporary Arts, London) is a piece of positive criticism in which he discusses a number of the potters in this book. Fritsch, McNicoll and Poncelet are named, and Britton's work implied, in a review of various 'inhibitions' to do with volume and surface and 'the extraordinary reluctance of many British potters to make compound, articulated shapes'. Rawson associates these problems with the prestigious example of Hans Coper's work. For Rawson, Coper was too much a silhouette-maker to want to deal with the full complexity of ceramic themes and metaphors, and so special ceramic inflections of volume, space, surface and that

6. Alison Britton
'White Jug with Spout' 1990 earthenware
width 20in (50cm)

7. Alison Britton
'Black Leaning Pot' 1990 earthenware
height 17in (44cm)

most mysterious quality 'presence' were not powerfully aided by his influence. But here are Rawson's own words on space and context:

> If you are going to make pieces expressly to support painting then both body and painting need to interact thematically and metaphorically, so that the contained pot space itself plays a part in the metamorphosis — else the piece just remains a funny object, not an utterance in a language, speech noise rather than poetry.
>
> And there is the question of space. How many pots in this [i.e. 'Fast Forwards'] exhibition genuinely 'take possession' of the three dimensions of space? It is not enough to say, 'It's an object, so it's bound to be three-dimensional'. The creator's proper job is to lead the spectator's attention to dwell in a space which is not that of the common world. To be a common thing in a common space – as Giacometti pointed out – is not expression.

I am not so sure. Rawson is always worth attending to; his *Ceramics* (1971, republished 1984) is now the classic text of pots as complex, concrete maps of life and action within a world of meaning. His strong emotional apprehension of any fully realized example of pottery, however commonplace, must induce that special heightened space – any thing of quality, however humdrum, must have its aura. Well, yes *and* no! His criteria are generous and conservative – perhaps 'conserving' is more precise; the values, the qualities are tuned to a universal synthesis of ceramic characteristics that might well have won the approval of Bernard Leach and Peter Fuller.

My friendly objection to Rawson, and to others who locate the key elements of meaning entirely *within* a specific art, is that such enclosure has in this century already led to a bleak formalism — many an -ism has perished from its own narrowing perfections: Purism, Constructivism, Minimalism. The crafts themselves – the *handicrafts* – were dangerously weakened by their yearning for their own past: they sought to preserve historic values within an aesthetic enclosure even though they had already been engulfed by modern industrially-based life. Michael Fried's well-known formulation of late Modernist belief (from his 1967 essay 'Art and Objecthood') now implies a similar wish to enclose, protect, preserve:

20

The concepts of quality and value – and to the extent that these are central to art, the concept of art itself – are meaningful...only *within* the individual arts. What lies *between* the arts is theatre.

Translated into artifacts this radical, reductionist claim traps art *inside* the practice of each art. Each object becomes an icon dedicated to the worship of itself – the dramas of human life as registered on the visual world of art are virtually ignored – *this* art talks only to itself. A supreme example of this is Frank Stella's famous remark about his own paintings: he wanted to keep the paint 'as good as it was in the can'. Speaking in 1968, Stella's words (and Freid's') supported the self-conscious purity of High Modernism at a time when Pop Art was cheerfully mixing and muddling diverse genres of representation.

In Britain, in the crafts, modes of representation had become a prime source for generating imagery at the close of the 1960s. Major changes during the decade in visual arts education had backfired, according to Reyner Banham who wrote gleefully in *Crafts* magazine that attempts to liberalize parts of the art school curriculum in order to turn students into Modernists had resulted in new generations of Historicists! As a critic of architecture and design, Banham was delighted by any impulse that might irritate and enliven the genteel world of British applied arts in which dull though worthy fact had always been honoured above frivolous (because usually *foreign*) fancy. The consequences for the crafts are still unravelling, but at the end of the 1960s the principal change in British work was a much greater awareness of the issues they shared with the other arts in other countries. The first beneficiaries of this quiet change of view and sensibilities were the *arts* of jewellery and pottery.

Pottery was the slower of the two activities to change, probably because it was thought to be more heavily encumbered with worthy and meaningful traditions. Craft potters of every kind inherited some version of their own imaginative history. It was not, is not, surprising that representation has so unavoidably shaped the humdrum as well as the fancifully, imaginatively conceived object. In most arts built on crafts the distinctions between fact and fancy are explained by the different ideas assigned to the functional or to the

8. Angus Suttie
'Your Tongue in My Cheek' 1990
earthenware width 22in (56cm)
(two views: below and on right)

9. Angus Suttie
Teapot 1986 earthenware
height 11in (29cm)

expressive. Many of this century's best artist-potters have tried to reunite the two sets of ideas within a single aesthetic.

But each set shines brightest on its own, although its ideas are greatly enhanced by an awareness of the counterpart ideas in the *other* set. Here, in praise of the humdrum, is 'The Kizaemon Teabowl', Yanagi's 1931 essay about a Korean pot enshrined for its ordinariness. Philosopher-aesthetician Yanagi (1889-1961) was a Japanese John Ruskin, friend and mentor of Bernard Leach and founder of the Japanese Folkcraft movement. He praised the teabowl as 'commonest crockery' and made a pilgrimage to see it be specially unwrapped from its layers of silk within a series of five boxes. This was his response:

> The plain and unagitated, the uncalculated, the harmless, the straightforward, the natural, the innocent, the humble, the modest: where does beauty lie if not in these qualities? The meek, the austere, the unornate – they are the natural characteristics that gain man's affection and respect. More than anything else, this pot is healthy.

Appropriately, the bowl was kept in a temple.

The alternative set of qualities can be found at work in Alison Britton's 1983 article in *Crafts* magazine, 'From Sèvres to Krazy Kat'. After ten years as a potter she said she was writing 'to look at the ornamental status of my kind of non-functional object'. The essay is a maker's description of formal strategies; where Yanagi colours his pot with moral absolutes, Britton owns up to relativities. Her written object has identikit features made up from the work of her admired peers (she mentions Fritsch, McNicoll, Woodman whose work is shown in this book, as well as other British and USA potters). This kind of artifact has not escaped from tradition – as she says, 'Our line of pot precedents, from Peasant to Industrial to Arts-and-Crafts to the Oriental Drift, is unavoidable and unforgettable for most potters, fencing themselves around with taboos and truth to materials.' – but it has transformed its sources by rewriting their terms of reference. The new pot is a gnarled hybrid: a decorative object that has recycled decoration and imagery to find its own form; a sophisticated object that features distortion and deception as formal devices; an object poised between the ordinary and the metaphorical and exhibiting some ambiguity of purpose.

These abstract vessels are doubtful objects: creatures of intricate process because they are respectful of archaic forms and the traces of ancient conventions, but they are also reconstructions of modern imaginings about such material. The ambiguity of purpose that Britton identifies invites the imagination to be categorical. What is it? *This* or *that?* Making objects which hold such questions in suspension can be a poetic act; not avoiding decision, but instead fancifully decorating and displaying it like gilding and garlanding the horns of your dilemma.

The abstract vessel comes to life when its conventions are stressed and dissected by a fierce and generous imagination. Without that break-and-make-it energy artifacts too easily become factual and formal question-posers – with the ready answer already prepared: a refined museum-flavoured reference nicely chunked and sauced as ornament.

Betty Woodman
Drawing of multiple forms 1987

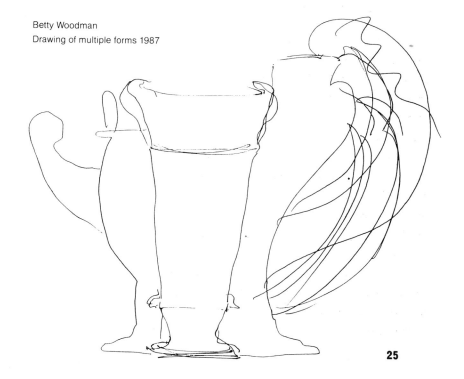

10. Angus Suttie
Bottle 1985 earthenware
height 18in (45cm)

11. Carol McNicoll
Fruit Dish 1990 earthenware width 17in (43cm)

"It is only when an object exists in our life for no other purpose than to be seen that we really look at it, as for instance a China ornament or a precious stone, and towards such even the most normal person adopts to some extent the artistic attitude of pure vision abstracted from necessity."

Roger Fry: *An Essay in Aesthetics* (1909)

Angus Suttie Drawing 1990

Abstraction and the vessel

Habit and humility have kept the functional pot normal and noble – at least that is its reputation within the image-conscious 'and-what-sort-of-pot-are-*you?*' world of the artist-crafts. Industrialisation saturated all markets with objects that quickly cornered the cheap and useful market. We have invented the hand-made post-industrial pot to try to recover qualities that only we have seen in those alien pre-industrial pots. We have our reasons that the makers of those pots probably never knew; our pots are flowers on their graves; they can never have revenge.

Our hand-made functional pots have also got fresh reasons for being like that: function has been redefined to suit our resonating sense of what such pots can be. Wittgenstein proposed that 'meaning is use' and much of the meaning in these objects represents the maker's wish to remember those 'older' qualities; function is an amalgam of that reimagining and the practical means of representing it – the making of both pot and meaning. All of our objects are swarming with such significance, but what signs will the future read in them? Probably the desire for romancing function.

The vessel is an abstraction that invites metaphor and a whole toyshop of language games; 'two-faced objects', as Alison Britton has discussed them, can combine aspects of prose and poetry; the 'action' of function entwined with decorative signs of contemplation and commentary. Britton's own pottery has been garlanded with her own written commentaries in catalogues

13. Carol McNicoll
Fruit Bowl 1989 earthenware width 22in (56cm)

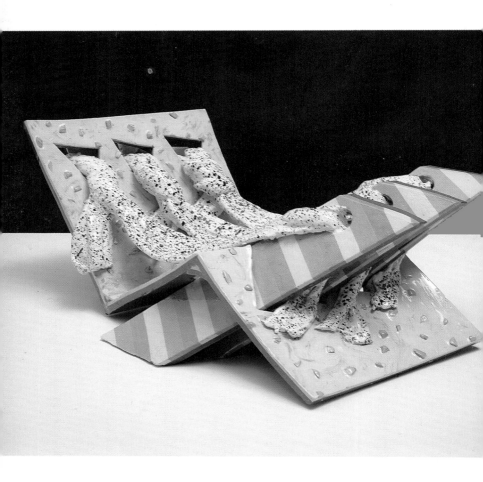

12. Carol McNicoll
Fruit Bowl 1981 earthenware width 19in (48cm)

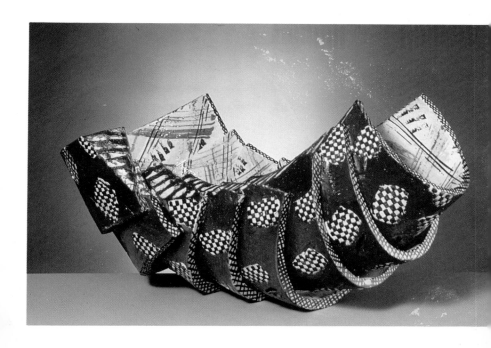

14. Carol McNicoll
Fruit Bowl 1983 earthenware height 9in (23cm)

and magazines – her sense of sharing a range of motives and meanings with other artist-craftspeople projects this writing as a general explanation: of her 'group' of Royal College graduates (classes of '68 to '70), of her own generation and the next (some of the latter taught by her at the Royal College),and of the genre.

Let the genre stand as the *idea* and the *image* of the vessel. Discussion of the genre most often and most usefully takes place in oracular terms; our modern oracles speak with the tongues of psychology, sociology and anthropology: 'rites of passage', 'alienation', 'representation' are words of power that quiver in the middle-class vocabularies of explanation and interpretation. These priestly functions permeate this genre. As Britton writes in 'The Maker's Eye', 'such objects stand back and describe, or represent, themselves as well as being'. In the same essay she tries to explain her 'inability to stop making vessels' and is thoughtfully, doubtfully eloquent about a cluster of reasons – the potter's training, potential use as justification, hiding from the purely aesthetic object. But, digging deeper, she suggests, 'Or I may have an irresistible (and fairly abstract) preoccupation with something very deep-rooted. Vessels are basic, archetypal, timeless. A container is a fundamental prop (and symbol) of civilization.' This well-stated motive implies its own origins in a kind of collective consciousness, not of forms, but of images and ideas. In his *Ceramics* Philip Rawson writes of 'the primal interweaving of matter, human action, and symbol that each pot represents'. For him, these objects fill the gap between life and art in ways which other arts – he cites painting and sculpture in particular – do not: they 'resemble cut flowers, separated from the living plant which produced them', whereas 'in the case of ceramics we are everywhere brought face to face with the root'. That image of an origin again. Rawson's passionate insights discover all of human life in each successful pot: nothing lost, all held in balance. He describes this as 'a "transformation image", something undeniably material, wearing the evidence of its material nature in its visible and tangible forms and attributes, which at the same time contains so much projected into it from man's daily life and experience at all levels that it can seem to him almost like a projection of his own bodily existence.'

This invocation of pottery's capacities, in a section of Rawson's book entitled 'The Existential Base', can be the keynote for much of the work illustrated in this book. These artists, having chosen to be potters, draw great strength from their sense of pottery past; for most of them the vessel has an honoured, ancestral role as a metaphor-rich site of fundamental qualities. It is Stonehenge, the Acropolis, Persepolis: each a site of mysterious and semi-mythical presence. In this century the container excites our imaginings at various levels; it is the ideal, the ur-form, even for those artists here, such as Baldwin and Eglin, who deploy closed, inaccessible forms. The vessel remains a central notion – possibly the primary one. As Primo Levi says:

> Man is a builder of receptacles; a species that does not build any is not human by definition. In short it seems to me that to fabricate a receptacle is due to two qualities which, for good or evil, are exquisitely human. The first is the ability to think about tomorrow...the second...is the capacity to foresee the behaviour of matter.

One reason why our twentieth-century imaginings can be so excited by pottery's capacity to measure or contain humanity's nature is the connection with creation myths. The abstract vessel is impregnated with our thoughts of raw clay as malleable as flesh, fired clay as persistent as memory...a glib romanticism *and* a reminder that The Potter and The Pot are archetypal elements in our Judaeo-Christian culture. No wonder our ceramic abstractions can support such lengthy commentaries; the oracles had a ready-made script.

Sixty years ago *the* word on pottery as abstraction came from an anarchist-atheist-poet who had been a Keeper in the Ceramics Department of the Victoria & Albert Museum. Herbert Read was a passionate spokesman for avant-garde art; in one of a series of radio talks (reprinted in 1931 as *The Meaning of Art*) he sympathetically interpreted pottery in terms derived from his master Wilhelm Worringer, whose *Abstraction and Empathy*, which was published in 1908, may have been a prime source for the development of abstraction in European art. And so 'will to form' and 'abstract essence' were broadcast as elements of *Art without Content*. The following passage from that talk has sometimes been appropriated to raise pottery's lowly aesthetic

15. Gordon Baldwin
'Vessel with Black Signs' 1990 earthenware
height 29in (74cm)

16. Gordon Baldwin
'Vessel with Dark Painting' 1990 earthenware
height 28in (71cm)

status; I am offering it as a point of view which is compatible with Rawson's richer conception.

Pottery is at once the simplest and the most difficult of all arts. It is the simplest because it is the most elemental; it is the most difficult because it is the most abstract. Historically it is among the first of the arts. The earliest vessels were shaped by hand from crude clay dug out of the earth, and such vessels were dried in the sun and wind. Even at that stage, before man could write, before he had a literature or even a religion, he had this art, and the vessels then made can still move us by their expressive form. When fire was discovered, and man learned to make his pots hard and durable; and when the wheel was invented, and the potter could add rhythm and uprising movement to his concepts of form,then all the essentials of this most abstract art were present. The art evolved from its humble origins until, in the fifth century before Christ, it became the representative art of the most sensitive and intellectual race that the world has ever known. A Greek vase is the type of all classical harmony. Then eastward another great civilization made pottery its best-loved and most typical art, and even carried the art to rarer refinements than the Greek had attained. A Greek vase is static harmony, but the Chinese vase, when once it had freed itself from the imposed influences of other cultures and other techniques, achieves dynamic harmony; it is not only a relation of numbers, but also a living movement. Not a crystal but a flower.

The perfect types of pottery, represented in the arts of Greece and China, have their approximations in other lands: in Peru and Mexico, in medieval England and Spain, in Italy of the Renaissance, in eighteenth-century Germany – in fact, the art is so fundamental, so bound up with the fundamental needs of civilization, that a national ethos must find its expression in this medium. Judge the art of a country, judge the fineness of its sensibility, by its pottery; it is a sure touchstone. Pottery is pure art; it is art freed from any imitative intention. Sculpture, to which it is most nearly related, had from the first an imitative intention, and is perhaps to that extent less free for the expression of the will to form than pottery; pottery is plastic art in its most abstract essence.

36

Philip Eglin
Drawing 1989

11·2·89

37

17. Gordon Baldwin
Two 'Developed Bottles' 1982
earthenware black height 24in (62cm)
white height 29in (75cm)

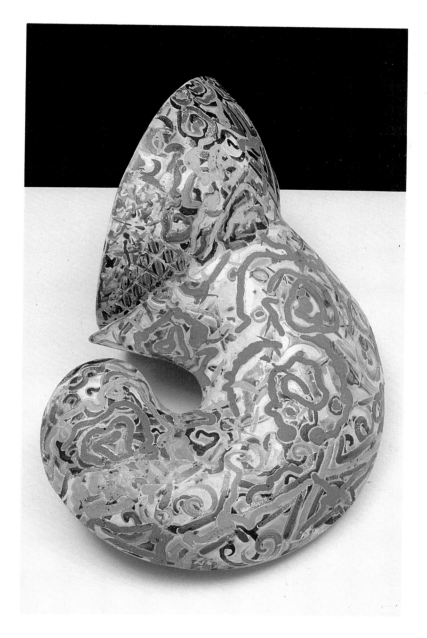

18. Gordon Baldwin
'Developed Bottle' 1982 earthenware
height 29in (75cm)

19. Jacqui Poncelet
'Openended Spiral' 1984 earthenware
height 29in (75cm)

*"I had already noticed in things a sort of
conspiratorial air. Was it to me that it was
addressed? I regretfully felt that I had no means
of understanding ... You could have sworn that
things were thoughts which stopped halfway,
which forgot themselves, which forgot what they
had wanted to think and which stayed like that,
swaying to and fro, with a funny little meaning
which went beyond them."*

Jean-Paul Sartre: *Nausea* (1938), translated by Robert Baldick

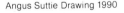
Angus Suttie Drawing 1990

The Thinking Object

Read and Rawson – even Alison Britton at times – they all express solidarity with an image of pottery which is unchanging, archetypal, fundamental. It's an image that each of them has constructed from inherited material: a legacy of theory and other fictions which we all share, more or less, as heirs to Modernism. That colossal project, unrealized by the middle of this century, has supplied our collective consciousness with its jumbled hopes and fears, with an alienated sense of history – 'the past is a foreign country, they do things differently there'. Not traditions, but myths made meaning plain; studies of the psyche shaped the singular arts; theories of social production led to revolution and mass consumption. At one extreme: industry, technology, design; the abstracted power that Octavio Paz calls 'the sign of a function'. But closer to us is the hand-made (this is from Paz's 1973 essay 'Use and Contemplation'). The hand-made shares our existence and our nature; even its ruins reflect our being. In its corporeal intimacy it is the sign of brotherhood.

The Paz essay appears in the World Crafts Council's *In Praise of Hands*, a big picture-book that tried to blend traditional artifacts with contemporary artist-crafts in order to celebrate some shared order of activity and to confirm a kind of continuity. But all of the pieces stayed separated. The vernacular objects, as always, were unbiddable: active objects at rest under the photographer's lights. The contemporary pieces were clamorous with explanations and individuality; lots of similar voices, but all trying to shout different messages. No doubts about meaning; every object was aesthetically agitated by the urgent need to express...something. Paz's essay understandably embraced the vernacular work, which he was eager to assimilate to his own life as a poet. And so his opening paragraph evokes such an object, conjures an abstract vessel as a container for his contemplation.

20. Jacqui Poncelet
'Interlocking Forms' 1986 earthenware
lengths 32 & 26in (83 & 67cm)

21. Jacqui Poncelet
'Horn and Claw' 1985 earthenware
length 42in (107cm)

22. Jacqui Poncelet
'Three Limbs and Tail' 1984 earthenware
length 34in (86cm)

Firmly planted. Not fallen from on high: sprung up from below. Ocher, the color of burnt honey. The color of a sun buried a thousand years ago and dug up only yesterday. Fresh green and orange stripes running across its still-warm body. Circles, Greek frets: scattered traces of a lost alphabet? The belly of a woman heavy with child, the neck of a bird. If you cover and uncover its mouth with the palm of your hand, it answers you with a deep murmur, the sound of bubbling water welling up from its depths; if you tap its sides with your knuckles, it gives a tinkling laugh of little silver coins falling on stones. It has many tongues: it speaks the language of clay and minerals, of air currents flowing between canyon walls, of washerwomen as they scrub, of angry skies, of rain. A vessel of baked clay: do not put it in a glass case alongside rare precious objects. It would look quite out of place. Its beauty is related to the liquid that it contains and to the thirst that it quenches. Its beauty is corporal: I see it, I touch it, I smell it, I hear it. If it is empty, it must be filled; if it is full, it must be emptied. I take it by the shaped handle as I would take a woman by the arm, I lift it up, I tip it over a pitcher into which I pour milk or pulque – lunar liquids that open and close the door of dawn and dark, waking and sleeping. Not an object to contemplate: an object to use.

I have quoted this passage in full because the poetic prose is dealing with the same formal and metaphorical problems as the contemporary objects in *that* book, published seventeen years ago. It was a time when the artist-crafts, especially those in North America, had become the vehicle for a self-conscious searching for new contexts and contents. Everybody seemed to find a different answer – by plundering the devices of twentieth-century art and transposing the imagery and methods of the many -isms into the material of their craft. As so often in the past, ceramics was the most prolific borrower, converting the art of the century into the ornaments of the 1970s. Because the transformation process was most often glib and technical, or cornily humorous, very few of these artifacts transcended their arbitrarily chosen origins. Although often technically elaborate – which attracted, and held, the viewer's attention – their presence as objects seldom clinched the contact. Examples? David Gilhooly's frog-centred narrative pieces; Richard Shaw's dazzling collages of cast found objects; and the most successful of the three, Ken Price's cup-like and container-like artifacts, leading up to 'De Chirico's Bathhouse' of 1980.

How did they escape the general mayhem of plagiarism? Each found a way to add some aesthetic density to their objects by inventing a context within their own lives. Each tried to escape from the familiar forms of pottery. The given language of plates and bowls and jugs was (and is) inflected with older social habits. Even after Voulkos (himself a national prizewinner at making bowls in the early 1950s) dramatized this pottery language as a gestural image, most potters still looked for simple precedents and adapted the images and stratagems of earlier avant-garde art as though it had been a common language. This common language was fatal to most artist-craftspeople's aims. When the source was evident, it hung on the new object like a stolen overcoat; when obscure, the reference irritated – like an incomplete phrase. Ken Price has always been master of his own phrasing: intensely reductive, his most abstract objects are autonomous object-poems. Their formal gloss is relieved by slight references beyond the abstraction; faint figurings of the organic, the historical, the personal. As Benny Green says of a jazz musician: 'He doesn't play a tune like *itself,* he plays it like *himself.'*

The object-poem is a dangerous genre: hybrid, bastard, and often appealing to the outer world for supportive reference. But, from within the hazily defined world of expressive objects, so do the potters in this book refer outside, wishing to acknowledge some aspect of a vernacular source, or a vital landscape, or a notion of vestigial function. My hope for these and for some other artist-potters is that we may discover where their objects can find their most complete expression. Peter Dormer's terrible and memorable phrase, that such artifacts 'thicken the middle-class environment' delivers these objects to the doctors, lawyers, architects and others, but seems to imply a Soames Forsythe response. Would Soames have understood a Gauguin pot? He owned one of the paintings. But these ceramic objects have a range of ambitions that goes far beyond the decorative and ornamental references in a Queen Anne silver chocolate pot or a Chinese Chippendale mirror frame; good examples of those older objects display the subtle fusion of several

45

23. Elizabeth Fritsch
'Mother and Child Ash Bottles (Blown Away)'
1990 stoneware greatest height 19in (48cm)

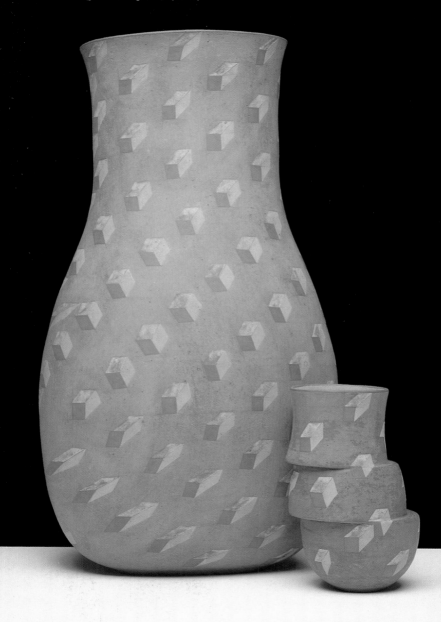

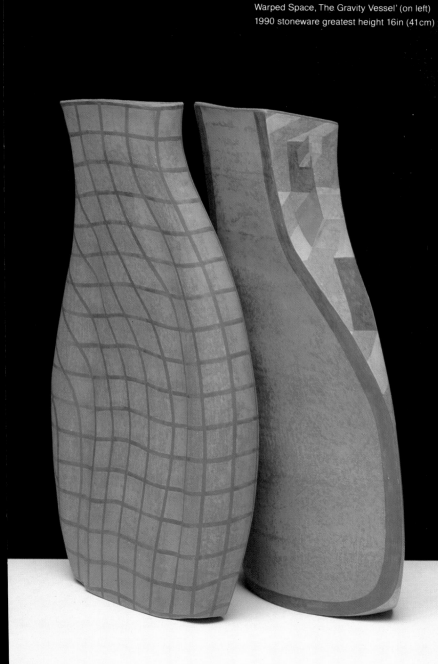

24. Elizabeth Fritsch
'Counterpoint Jar (on right) with Its Shadow of
Warped Space, The Gravity Vessel' (on left)
1990 stoneware greatest height 16in (41cm)

separate skills, but the quality of every mark is as narrowly controlled as the movements in dressage or championship ballroom dancing. Soames would have understood. In that excellent essay 'Gaugin, Ceramics and Decorative Meaning' by Edward Allington, he writes of the beginning of this century as the time when 'decoration became merely decorative in its modern somewhat derogatory sense of the word; all embedded iconographic meaning became sublimated to the desires of the newly powerful merchant classes'. He proposes that 'decoration with iconographic meaning is dependent on a coherent structure of poetic thought which underpins and connects the references and allusions made within the decorative form'.

Poetic thought is the plateau on which all these objects stand. With one exception all the forms and all the decoration is abstract; and yet the iconography is fairly clear (clearer than the signs and symbols of Christianity are to most Christians) just because it is tuned to the genres of Modernist abstraction. So Eastman's broad polychrome geometrics have a New City optimism on his primal, monumental forms. Baldwin's monochrome structures are complex elisions of body and landscape: tiny emphatic marks and embossed grids overlay rolling heroic forms; signs of decoration and investigation in a probing archaeology of Modernism.

There is a decorative, reconstructive process at work within the poetry. The potter's affectionate loyalty to pottery's conventions has tended in the West to keep opinion on the surface. Post-Renaissance (meaning time *and* culture) pots of high degree delivered complicated pictorial messages which the potters mostly did not understand; they reproduced and adapted and sometimes muddled the classical imagery that had been designed by higher status artists who got the stories from highest status poets. But an artist-potter has to understand, and represent the whole process through all of the appropriate levels, from infra-structure to metaphysics. Just to quote and permutate can produce exhilarating objects: our senses are so in love with meaning (and our own consciousness of it) that the decorative and the ornamental are read as signs of generosity; pattern's rhythmic repetitions soothe and stimulate. No thing can escape our contemplative search for meaning (see Yanagi, see Paz, see Sartre's hero, elsewhere in this book) but objects that are consciously and entirely made from meaning enjoy special difficulties. The meaning may be too private; the nature of the genre may interfere; nobody is interested. The meaning may matter less than the marks it leaves. Source, intention, motive are all circumstantial evidence; they may be describable, discussable facts but the artifact is shaped and patterned by the pressure of belief, not by the small print. Elizabeth Fritsch, in twenty years of working, has acknowledged the importance of visionary beliefs as sustaining forces: sustaining and enriching the relations that she has eloquently described between the physical and the metaphysical elements which form her pots. It's not just a question of inspirational texts. We are all fans of those whose words genuinely free our imagination, but seldom become their disciples. Fritsch has found ways to translate admiration into action, and contrariwise to invoke complex theory from disparate fields – theatre, music, literature, and most recently physics – to animate her complex representations of space and pattern. Some sense of allegory has always pervaded this patterning: the marks measure equivalences, intervals, illusions. Decoration is pierced by meaningful structures. The marks measure abstracted meaning; the underlying forms are significantly infinite and innocent before they are caught in their topographical nets.

Forms as organisms, marks as meaning portrayed (or dissembled) are the animating analogies for the thinking object. The organism can be read as building – as with Britton, Eastman, but it is flagrantly a personal space that is being idealized. McNicoll and Fritsch read themselves into intricate structures; Fritsch making them precious and poised, McNicoll stacking and sorting her mimetic components with a decorative crackle of witty calculation. I exaggerate a little, but I believe that the analogy can bear it: ceramic form(s) are invested with organic and psychological attributes; they partially represent 'body' in a wide range of weakish metaphors that carry our thoughts from something corporeal and active to imagined attributes of the spiritual and the contemplative. At one extreme – the ornament, the counterpart of utility; an idea made precious by being concentrated in a symbol; a single-minded object. At the other extreme – which is almost off the edge of the ceramic map–there is the thinking object, a newish hybrid still in an ambi-

25. Elizabeth Fritsch
'Funerary Jar, with Spout Pot and Drinking Cup
(from Tlön)' 1990 stoneware greatest height
13in (33cm)

26. Ken Eastman
Pot 1991 stoneware height 14in (35cm)

27. Ken Eastman
Pot 1990 stoneware width 14in (36cm)

guous stage of evolution. A fictional object whose makers – these and some other artist-potters – have long and loyal memories of their craft. It is these memories, intensified and reimagined through the strategies of this century's arts, that play across the features of these extraordinary artifacts.

Memory is both the artist's raw material and the mesh through which experience sifts. I find it hard to accept that different arts may be fundamentally distinct just because they differ at the sifting, sorting level. It is, at least partly, the reflection of the Modernist argument that quality and value are only meaningful *within* the individual arts. And so . . . there is a powerful etiquette which governs manners in each art, and manners maketh memory; at least, manners speak to memory. All this a preamble to the problem of Jacqui Poncelet's ceramics. It's important to say that it's not her problem, that when her artifacts reached a categorical edge (of material, of vesselhood) they vanished from the bounded world of hand-made ceramics. In this book she is represented by ceramics made in the 1980s. 1985 being her last year as a wholly ceramic presence. For most of her career until then she had been a vessel-maker, of an ornamental and increasingly metaphorical sort. The idea of ornament and the suffusing, transforming power of decoration became analogues for bodily sensations. In David Ward's words, 'Combined embossed textures on the body of a form were painted in a complexity of patterned marks, producing the sense that every point on the surface had been touched.' Although Poncelet's ceramic forms clearly stated their hollowness, her formal analogies no longer agreed with the pot as container. Her elongating artifacts became tubes, horns, limbs: they were free objects that could be stood, leaned, and balanced in a variety of ways. Their ornamental, ceramic nature had become a site for unpredictable, formally unstable analogies. In her own words: 'how to assimilate the alien via the artifice of the object?'

There has been much talk of familiar forms in praising and defending the newer ceramic arts: it has been suggested that pottery's large audience is guaranteed by that familiarity. But, in truth, can you find familiar forms in the objects illustrated in this book? All abstract vessels, certainly, and in potters' terms referable to precedent. Even Eglin's figures are described by him as 'vessels'; as creatures of the hollowish breed, still the prime criterion for keeping faith with their past. His figures are subtly developed, from his own vigorous drawings from life, from painting, from sculpture, from pottery figurines. But his objects' meanings rise out of the tough reimaginings of representation; meanings confirmed by the daub and drip of 'added' decoration which aligns a modern vandal vernacular of splodged graffiti with the innocent splashes of older painting on pots.

Betty Woodman's brilliance as painter-potter-representer does take her close to familiar simple forms, to the rolling, glowing patterned vernaculars of folk pottery from Mexico, Italy, Greece. Her image-objects confront the viewer with a definite composition (sometimes there is a different 'front' view on the other side of such an object) which suggests a whole or partial silhouette of a pot that has been captured and camouflaged by its own surroundings. The fixed overlap and viewpoint create pictorial expectations, but these are strongly modified by the vigour of outline or jut of bas-relief. The mutual tug of the overlapping systems sets up a sense of movement, something happening within the image — a fleeting, sentient quality.

That sense of activity *within* the object — not just the lure of usefulness which invites activity, to grip a handle, tip a jug — but forms defined as a portrayal of their own logic, is best created by *unfamiliar* forms. Unfamiliar, at least, to the ceramic repertoire. Woodman creates one clear expectation of edge or pattern, then cuts into it with another, equal strength, visual clue. Her dynamic juxtapositions are pictorial and optical. But the classic clashes of this century are the psychic collisions of Surrealist practices: head-on incongruity, or the slither and spikes of nightmare biologies. In this book, Gordon Baldwin has once been a most studied practitioner of Surreal and Dada strategies. The resonant nature of his artifacts' formal language is transmitted by subtle confluences of clues alluding to biology and geology: suggestive of difference, of similarity, of a sentient *place.*

Angus Suttie, like Baldwin, respects the random, the fortuitous, the worrying, as personal messages. His artifacts evolve from a few happy meetings among a range of pre-made forms; forms made without prior knowledge of the meetings. As the work grows he tends its needs with an affectionate surprise; discovering decisions about which way is up, the possibility of a leg or a

28. Ken Eastman
Pot 1990 stoneware height 16in (40cm)

handle, the likelihood of a lid, or orifices. All this in the combined light of Surrealism and folk art. The folk are often and importantly South American: the anthropomorphic multi-chambered smooth but clenched vessels are one sort. The Surreal is now one of this century's ways to say Nature, and to mean the world inside. The vocabularies of a real life that is, that has to be, totally invented, are better said in visual images than in words. These secret forms are not familiar, but we know them from our sleeping and waking dreams. They are ourself. Suttie's objects are in tune with that waking-dreaming: literally sensation, memory, wishful thinking − not described, but *embodied*. It is now the feelings that are familiar, though none the less mysterious. The process of embodiment is also familiar, mysterious, and, as John Updike describes the process in *Self-consciousness,* his 1989 memoir, deep-rooted in a primitive hope for understanding:

> I had propelled my body through the tenderest parts of a town that was also somewhat my body. Yet my pleasure was innocent and my hope was primitive. I had expected to be told who I was, and why, and had not been entirely disappointed.

That image of the body as the prime analogy of a form to render feeling is what transforms the abstract vessel into the thinking object. In ceramics it is still a hesitant and intricate process, but it seems to me that it is the most aesthetically promising direction for potters such as these. It is extraordinarily demanding: familiar forms have to be made over, to become capable of poetic reference; a reimagining of functions is part of the modern conception of such individual artifacts. The idea of the useful object as slave or servant, at best an obedient helper in specialized action, has been absorbed by other images, other ways such objects can please us, serve us. Octavio Paz has shown how we transform such objects − old as well as new-made − to remake them closer to ourselves, to mingle their nature with our own. That assimilation is an ancient process: Ovid wanted 'To speak of bodies transformed into figures of different kinds.' Images of change, of feeling transforming substance, of the play of our thoughts transfiguring raw materials; that is the wish fulfilled in these thinking objects.

Publications

Arranged as two separate lists: the first, for books; the other, for exhibition catalogues and periodicals. These amplify the references in the biographies. Books are listed alphabetically by author. In the other list, catalogues are identified from the name of their publishing institution, and periodicals under their own title. For example: Dormer (1986) refers to Peter Dormer's book *The New Ceramics;* Crafts Council (1979) to *The Work of Alison Britton,* the catalogue of her retrospective exhibition.

Books

Birks, Tony 1976 *The Art of the Modern Potter*
Clark, Garth 1981 *American Potters: The Work of Twenty Modern Masters*
   1988 *American Ceramics: 1876-Present*
Dormer, Peter 1985a *Alison Britton in Studio* (with David Cripps)
   1985b *Elizabeth Fritsch in Studio* (with David Cripps)
   1986 *The New Ceramics: Trends and Traditions*
Lucie-Smith, Edward 1975 *The World of the Makers*
Rawson, Philip 1984 *Ceramics*
Rice, Paul and Gowing, Christopher 1989 *British Studio Ceramics
   in the Twentieth Century*
Watson, Oliver 1990 *British Studio Pottery: the Victoria and
   Albert Museum Collection*
Wechsler, Susan 1981 *Low-Fire Ceramics: a new Direction in American Clay*
Yanagi, Soetsu 1972 *The Unknown Craftsman,* which includes his 1931 essay 'The
   Kizaemon Tea-Bowl'; all adapted by Bernard Leach

Catalogues and Periodicals

Art in America, NY, USA 1990 November 'From Function To Form' by Janet Koplos,
   on new work by Betty Woodman
Boymans-van Beuningen Museum, Rotterdam, Netherlands 1989
   Mysterieuze Volumes catalogue of an exhibition of new work by Gordon Baldwin,
   essay by Dorris Kuyken-Schneider

30. Philip Eglin
'Olympia in Blue after Manet' 1986
earthenware width 24in (61cm)

31. Philip Eglin
'Reclining Nude' 1990 earthenware
width 20in (50cm)

32. Philip Eglin
'Standing Female Nude'
1986 earthenware
height 24in (61cm)

Ceramic Review, London 117-1989 'Traditions' by Angus Suttie

Cleveland County Museum Service, Middlesbrough 1982 *Gordon Baldwin:* a retrospective view 1954-82 essay by John Houston

Contemporary Applied Arts, London 1990 *Sara Radstone and Angus Suttie* exhibition leaflet essay by Alison Britton

Crafts Council, London 1979 *The Work of Alison Britton* catalogue with essay by John Houston and other contributions

    1981a *Jacqui Poncelet: New Ceramics* catalogue with essay by Richard Deacon

    1981b *The Maker's Eye* catalogue with essays by 14 selectors

    1985 *Carol McNicoll: Ceramics* catalogue with essays by Oliver Watson and Richard Deacon

Crafts 51-1981 'Upstart Forms' by Tony Birks

    61-1983 'Sèvres with Krazy Kat' by Alison Britton

    88-1987 'Structural Logic' by Peter Dormer

    97-1989 'Notes on Time' by Elizabeth Fritsch

    98-1989 'The Critic's Eye' by Alison Britton

    102-1990 'The Venus of Harlow New Town' by Rosemary Hill

    104-1990 'Sara Radstone and Angus Suttie' by Tanya Harrod

    106-1990 Comment 'Six of the Best' by Rosemary Hill

        'Towers of Strength' by Tanya Harrod

Hetjens-Museum, Düsseldorf, Germany 1990 *Gordon Baldwin* catalogue of new work, essay in German by Ekkart Klinge

Institute of Contemporary Arts, London 1985 *Fast Forward: New Directions in British Ceramics* essays by Peter Dormer and others relating to exhibition with this title

Leeds Art Galleries 1978 *Pots About Music* essays relating to exhibition with this title of work by Elizabeth Fritsch

Museum Het Kruithuis, s'Hertogenbosch, Netherlands 1985 *British Ceramics* catalogue with essays by John Houston and others

Northern Centre for Contemporary Art, Sunderland 1987 *2D/3D: Art and Craft Made and Designed for the Twentieth Century* essays relating to exhibition with this title

Orchard Gallery, Londonderry, Northern Ireland 1983 *Fifty-Five Pots and Three Opinions* essays by Peter Dormer, Martina Margetts and Peter Fuller relating to exhibition with this title

Studio Yearbook of Decorative Art in Modern Interiors, London 1974-75; 1976-77; 1980 illustrated section on studio pottery

Biographies

Gordon Baldwin

Born 1932 in Lincoln, where he studied painting, then ceramics at the Central School of Art and Design, London, until 1954. His art is an extraordinary archaeology of Modernism. Like Donatello, he is archaizing an admired past. The archaizer steps out of time present for complex reasons, which include an imaginative affinity with a past *and* a proud desire to do it all again, but *my* way. He and Hans Coper are good examples of this creative dance through time: the thoughtful step backward adding power to the daring forward leap. Baldwin's artifacts, like Coper's tersely aspiring vessels, portray hope in the forms of a poetic sensibility. Despite the backward glance there are new forms and new feelings concerned with vessel-body-landscape insights. And some special force is supplied from that abstract landscape of the mind (pre-Christian, post-Freud) which is shared with heroes such as Arp, Duchamp, Brancusi, Moore... Good coverage of recent work in Boymans (1989) and Hetjens (1990); good words and pictures in Birks (1976) and, also by Birks, in *Crafts* (51-1981). Cleveland (1982) is retrospective, with an essay by me.

Alison Britton

Born 1948 in London, studied ceramics at Central School of Art and Design and Royal College of Art, both in London, until 1973. As potter, teacher, writer on the applied arts she has become the very image of the contemplative artist-potter, able to translate and explain the nature of such objects. As − in Northern (1987) − 'Novels have been written that consist of language as their subject matter as well as the material they are made from. Other arts have turned inward to look at their own rules too in this last half of the twentieth century. Pots have been made in the last decade or more that are looking at what a pot consists of. This is a respectful and not an anarchic process.' In the 1970s her facetted artifacts were incised and painted with a gently quizzical psychological repertoire: flowers and fish, trees and roots, birds and humans; all drifting by, or caught up in patterns on the wall-like surfaces of her (mostly) jugs. In the 1980s, form became bold and complex; decoration was dense and abstract; a darkening thicket of Pollockish trails and swirls. Most recently, the objects seem to be more single-minded and the decoration (less trails, more brushstrokes) more unified as marks, as tone. Good, different coverage in Crafts Council (1979), Dormer (1985a), and Harrod (1990), all with David Cripps' eloquent photographs. Harrod lists publications both *about* the artist and *by* her. Recommended: Britton's essay in Crafts Council (1981b), the classic 'Sévres with Krazy Kat' in *Crafts* (61-1983), and her introduction to the forthcoming *International Crafts Yearbook*, edited by Martina Margetts.

Ken Eastman

Born 1960 in Watford, studied ceramics in Edinburgh and the Royal College of Art, London, until 1987. He makes abstract vessels with a relished architectural significance, which seem to me to be concerned with the interior/exterior nature of human space – as 'a place for the eye to wander in' but also as a place for habitation. Too small to enter? But these are analogizing projects which reveal Eastman as an optimist of the New Modernist tendency. I propose 'domain' in addition to 'container'. Nominally 'pot', each object has a built order of being: description needs a vocabulary of walls, floor, roof; the painted slips and oxides of these matt surfaces connect with 'deteriorating fresco, or old walls where one layer of paint is partly visible through another...somehow these are building colours, faded in bright light.' In the same passage, Alison Britton mentions 'the fine distinction to be maintained, or else something that is simply a little clay model of a building will result.' So, let them be pots; but they are pots built with an ambiguous poetics of space in which I sense a complex urge to synthesize the two great (and kindred) communal arts that employ earth and stone to enclose spaces – in order to lay claim to them as *places*. Quotations from 'The Critic's Eye' in *Crafts* (98-1989), and an article by Tanya Harrod in *Crafts* (106-1990).

Philip Eglin

Born 1959 in Gibraltar, studied ceramics at Staffordshire Polytechnic and the Royal College of Art, London, until 1986. His bold painting abstracts these figures from their historic contexts. In a broad technical sense they are part of the ornamental vessel tradition. In two appreciative essays, in *Crafts* (102-1990) and (106-1990), Rosemary Hill has pointed to Eglin's Madonnas and Venuses as still connected to the folk pottery tradition, and able to work within it because we

still have affectionate memories of Staffordshire figurative groups and the slimmer flatback ornaments. In her words, 'we have an iconography and this is it. Its features are a little indistinct, there are some obvious joins and latterly vandalism and neglect, through which the meaning now appears. But it is ours and so we love it.' But his figures are much more than quotes from pottery and Cranach's paintings. They are vitally nourished by his own references; he draws from the nude with a searching vigour that jostles into life his canny borrowings. His painting tunes these objects to both old and new decoration: the cheerful colour splashes of eighteenth-century wares are extemporized as vandal daubs, and also serve as form-following brush strokes.

Elizabeth Fritsch

Born 1940 in Wales, studied at the Royal Academy of Music, London, and four years later studied ceramics at the Royal College of Art, London, until 1971. Her 1974 exhibition, at the Crafts Advisory Committee's London Gallery in 1974, was a major event. Here was an assured and complex range of artifacts: matt stonewares with geometric decoration of a slow, sonorous beauty. Some archaizing pieces, and newer work already 'inhabiting the shadowy space half-way between two and three dimensions'. She wrote about her work with a resounding clarity and conviction, as in Leeds (1978), where she cited early loves for 'Geometry, Classical Music, especially Bach, and Ancient History, especially Greek Mythology with its airy Mountain landscape'. She has faced the problem, which Gombrich stated as the most serious one to exist in the relation between music and the visual arts, of where does metaphor end, and analogy begin? In her referential Pantheon, Borges has joined William Blake, Piero della Francesca, Walter Benjamin...and, most recently *Superforce* (Paul Davies' 1984 book) with its references to Einsteinian geometry in which gravity becomes a manifestation of the curvature of space-time. All, somehow, touches the pots. Another essay by Fritsch in *Crafts* (97-1989); critical words from Philip Rawson in Institute of Contemporary Arts (1985); more sympathetic views in Lucie-Smith (1975) and Dormer (1985b) and Dormer (1986).

Carol McNicoll

Born 1943 in Birmingham, studied painting at Leeds Polytechnic and ceramics at the Royal College of Art, London, until 1973. Her virtuoso manipulations of techniques of slip-casting have assisted semi-industrial production runs of some pieces. Can the thinking object exist in replica? Probably not. It might undermine our confidence in thought as individual. Fortunately for me, only she can make her most individual pieces. So the multiples exist as 'one-liners' – sharp enough to bear repetition as wise-cracks about making an illusory object. The singly-made pieces are much more intricately constructed (and more sardonic, as they seem to me) and can therefore afford a richer range of reference to materials and methods. But replication is still the root of this art. The sculptor Richard Deacon writes, 'it seems to me that it is the notions of derivation, borrowing and replication inherent in casting that constitute continuity, coherence and the means of progression in Carol's work'. Deacon's essay, in Crafts Council (1985) is a fascinating appreciation

of the referential vibrations between making and meaning, 'a joining together of things we recognise with an awareness of something made, within a rich and beautiful surface'. Also helpful: Institute of Contemporary Arts (1985) and Dormer (1986). McNicoll is singled out by Peter Fuller, in Orchard Gallery (1983) as 'one of the worst, and regrettably among the most fashionable' of 'the "Krazy Kat" generation'.

Jacqui Poncelet

Born 1947 in Liège, Belgium, studied ceramics at Wolverhampton and at the Royal College of Art, London, until 1972. I remember an early and alarmingly delicate oval bowl with a three-dimensional fringe of geese. Glossy white and precious, it was like a Lucie Rie with Kate Greenaway topping. From there to the 'Interlocking Forms' of 1986 shown in this book now seems to have been a completed phase in a tough-minded career. She now makes work outside the practice of ceramics. But she still teaches this practice and I know numbers of students who see these last pieces of her pottery as still indicating the necessary dangerous path. The abstract vessel was always her mode of formal decorative development. In 1975 she stopped making the translucent cast and carved bone china vessels that were widely admired and copied. The next objects were slabby earthenware containers: taste-wise a switch from meringue to soggy cardboard, but leading to the complex and exhilarating vessels in her major exhibition – Crafts Council (1981a). Poncelet has always employed decoration as a navigational grid: to assimilate information, generate form, and reconcile the two. It led her towards the

63

body, to identify it as receptacle/vessel and as receiver/surface/skin to be marked. The reference above has an important essay by Richard Deacon; Institute of Contemporary Arts (1985) and Museum Het Kruithuis (1985) are also interesting.

Angus Suttie

Born 1946 in Tealing, Scotland, studied ceramics at Camberwell School of Arts and Crafts, London, until 1979.

Acknowledging his 'two seemingly irreconcilable influences' of Folk Art and Surrealism he composes artifacts that theatrically exceed the lengthy sum of their many pottery parts. Some of the graspable bits are inexplicably alien *and* ordinary; apparently derived from emblematic animal-haunted vessels from Central America. Suttie has a way of abstracting something of the gait and stance of such vessels: something precise about angle, scale and silhouette which gives a worrying credibility to the larger romping improvised event which is each object. The analogy for this event is, frankly, the body; a Surreal version with bumps, holes and overlaps rearranged in dream-like conjunctions. The Central Americans help here as well, fecundly suggestive of unfamiliar forms and unpredictably tiny orifices. All together, an object is a brilliant mish-mash of emblem, psychic flagrance and fastidiousness.

An interesting essay by Peter Dormer *Crafts* (88-1987). Contemporary Applied Arts (1990) and *Crafts* (104-1990) are discussions of Suttie in the same exhibition; words, respectively, by Alison Britton and Tanya Harrod. Suttie's own version is in *Ceramic Review* (117-1989), and, interviewed by his nom-de-plume Aeschylus Orton, in Museum Het Kruithuis (1985).

Betty Woodman

Born 1930 in Norwalk, Connecticut, USA, studied ceramics at the School for American Craftsmen at Alfred University, New York, from 1948 to 1950. The key word, and quality, is 'ease'; she uses it herself, and so do all who write about her objects. There is a fluency in the relation between the different stages in each piece. The layers — of body, added forms and straps and ribands, and painted colour and pattern — remain distinct; not separate, but visible through each other as through a frame. To look (and concentrate) is to have these levels shift and fluctuate; an imaginative process as well as an optical event. These inter-relations have provided the affirmative quality which is the spirit of her work; a kind of happy pantheism in which pottery is a whole world. Speaking about living in New Mexico, she said, 'Once again I found myself in an atmosphere, like Italy, where everything is made out of clay.' Her most recent pieces, in this book, have found new ways to overlay and to integrate the elements of her vision. On the cover, and inside are the two views of a single object 'Still Life Vase #6'; the object is essentially a free-standing cut-out in the centre of which a tallish vase form has become implicated, camouflaged, by vigorous painted scrolls and dabs and bars. These fall across the whole form, contradicting it, and being contradictorily cut off at the object's edges. Three levels that co-exist: voluminous pot; two-dimensional silhouette; overwhelming decoration. Janet Koplos has written about this recent work in *Art in America* (November 1990); good interview in Wechsler (1981) and helpful material in Clark (1981) and Clark (1988).